Immanuel Haller

Chosen But Free

How divine sovereignty relates to the human will

GRIN Verlag

Bibliografische Information der Deutschen Nationalbibliothek:

Die Deutsche Bibliothek verzeichnet diese Publikation in der Deutschen National-
bibliografie; detaillierte bibliografische Daten sind im Internet über http://dnb.d-
nb.de/ abrufbar.

Imprint:

Copyright © 2010 GRIN Verlag GmbH
Druck und Bindung: Books on Demand GmbH, Norderstedt Germany
ISBN: 978-3-656-23862-1

This book at GRIN:

http://www.grin.com/en/e-book/196284/chosen-but-free

CONTINENTAL THEOLOGICAL SEMINARY

CHOSEN BUT FREE –
HOW DIVINE SOVEREIGNTY RELATES TO THE HUMAN WILL

An essay prepared
For the course:
Anthropology / Hamartiology / Angelology

by
Immanuel Haller

Brussels, Belgium
Semester 2, May 2010

TABLE OF CONTENTS

INTRODUCTION

Did God decide that certain specific persons would go to heaven or hell, before he created the world? Did God know everything that would ever happen before he created anything? If so, did God know this because he determined these things would happen, or vice versa?[1] These, and similar questions have concerned Christians for centuries and raise the question of human responsibility to accept or reject the good news of the gospel.

In short, the aim of this essay is to develop a Pentecostal-Evangelical doctrine of election referring to the statement: "Man is ... entirely responsible to accept or reject the grace of God."

Firstly, one pictures divine sovereignty and how it relates to human free will. Here the writer also includes the question of the origin of evil. Secondly, there is a brief overview about the concepts of Calvinism, Pelagianism and Arminianism and a consideration of how much human will is affected by the fall. Lastly, the writer discusses the question of election and determines how this relates to human personal freedom of decision.

The limitation of words leaves no place for a historical-theological explanation or an indepth discussion about the concept of election. The writer simply derives that a significant free will goes to the heart of Christian anthropology and therefore man is entirely responsible for his decisions.[2]

---

[1] Chad Owen Brand, ed. *Perspectives on Election: 5 Views* (Nashville, TN: Broadman & Holman Publishers, 2006), 342.
[2] R.C. Sproul, *Willing to believe: The Controversy over Free Will* (Grand Rapids, MI: Baker Books, 1997), 28.

CHOSEN BUT FREE

Free Will or Divine Sovereignty

God's Sovereignty

The Bible illustrates a God who is before all things, beyond all things, creates all things, upholds all things, knows all things, can do all things and is ultimately in control of all things.[3] This complete control of all things is called the sovereignty of God. A careful study of scriptures shows, that even human decisions are under God's control.[4]

However, if God is in complete control of everything, including human choice, then how can man be truly free? Are not sovereignty and significant free will mutually exclusive? To put the problem another way, if God is in control of all events, then how can man be responsible for anything that happens, including his evil actions? Step by step man attempts to discover an answer to these unknowns.

Who Made the Devil Do?

Some excuse their sin, claiming: "The devil made me do it!" However, the problem is even greater, because logically one cannot stop at this point. For if God is in sovereign control of all things, then instead it would appear that, ultimately, "God made me do it."

Indeed one response to the problem of divine sovereignty and human responsibility is that of strong Calvinism.[5] This response claims that free choice is simply doing as one desires, but man does not desire to act unless God gives him the desire to do so.[6] In the end, one arrives at the crucial question; who caused Lucifer to sin? A logical Calvinistic deduction is (if all desires come from God) then God made Lucifer sin against God![7]

---

[3] Normen L. Geisler, *Chosen but free: A Balanced view of divine election* (Grand Rapids, MI: Baker Publishing Group, 2001), 14.

[4] See exemplary: Eph. 1:11, Rom. 8:29-30, Eph. 1:4, Acts 2:23, Acts 13:48, John. 1:13, Romans 9:16, Isaiah 8:14, 1 Peter 2:8, …

[5] Speaking about strong Calvinism one refers to the theology summarized in: "total depravity, unconditional predestination, limited atonement, irresistible grace, and the perseverance of the saints."

[6] Geisler, 20.

[7] Ibid, 21.

Who Made the Devil?

Here the writer argues that God did not make the devil, and He did not make the devil do it (sin). Rather, God made a good angel called Lucifer, who became the devil by his own free choice to sin. Therefore, in that case, his original evil act was self-caused, that is, caused by himself – which is exactly the view of human free will the strong Calvinist rejects.[8] Otherwise, one would argue that God could be against Himself, but God is essentially good. He cannot sin and does not tempt anyone to sin (Heb. 6:18 / James 1:13).

The Origin of Evil

One of the things God gave His good creatures was a good power called free will. God said to Adam: "You are free ... "(Gen. 2:16). Therefore, the power of moral free choice entails the ability to either choose the good God designed for man or to reject it. The latter is called evil. It is good to be free, but freedom makes evil possible. In short, free choice is the origin of evil.

Reward and Punishment

God is morally accountable for giving the good thing called free will, but He is not morally responsible for all the evil man does with his freedom. Praise or blame as man sees it in scripture, but also from common moral wisdom, makes no real sense unless those praising or blaming were free to do otherwise. The Bible clearly shows, that God holds humanity morally responsible, both prior to and after the Fall of Adam. From this viewpoint, the writer concludes that man must have a significant free will. Without a functional will, man's moral agency would perish and he would be reduced to a sham, a mere chimera with no substantive reality.[9]

---

[8] Ibid, 21.
[9] Sproul, 28.

4

Free Will and Divine Sovereignty

The writer briefly demonstrated that God is sovereign over all things, including human events and free choices. On the other hand, the writer has concluded that human beings, even in their fallen state, have the God-given power of free choice.[10] The writer is convinced that the mystery of the relationship between divine sovereignty and human free will, will not be solved by sacrificing human responsibility in order to preserve divine sovereignty (strong Calvinist position); nor by scarifying God's sovereignty in order to hold on to man's free will (left wing Arminianism). One must simply assume that from God's perspective total divine control and human responsibility are compatible.[11] To conclude otherwise would place human understanding above divine revelation. However, relating the essay question, the writer concludes, thus far, that Gods sovereignty does not exclude a significant free will.

---

[10] The effect of the fall see page 5-7.

[11] David Basinger and Randall Basinger, eds. *Predestination & Free Will* (Downers Grove, IL: InterVarsity Press, 1986), 11.

Seeing the Alternatives

Calvinism

Calvinists emphasise the concept of total depravity: every individual is so sinful as to be unable to respond to any offer of grace. They argue that man is free to come to God but not able. God in his sovereign will or good pleasure, however, elected certain individuals out of fallen humanity to receive eternal life.[12] Only the elected, when God comes in his special grace, are able to respond. Election, and therefore salvation, is unconditional and does not depend upon human beings performing a specific action or meeting certain conditions or terms of God. In short, those whom God has chosen will necessarily come to receive eternal life, because His election is from all eternity and immutable.[13]

Some Calvinists argue for a double predestination, the belief that God chooses some to be saved and others to be lost. Others argue that God actively chooses those who are to receive eternal life, and passes by all the others, leaving them in their self-chosen sins.[14]

Pelagianism

Pelagius strongly emphasized the idea of free will. As a moralist: his primary concern was for people to live good and decent lives. According to his view, Adam's sin has no direct effect upon every human being; there is no need for a special working of God's Grace within the heart of each individual. By their own efforts, they are perfectly able to fulfil God's commands without sinning.[15]

---

[12] Millard J. Erikson, *Introducing Christian Doctrine,* ed.R. Arnold Hustad (Grand Rapids, MI: Backer Academic, 2005), 300.

[13] Brand, 11.

[14] Augustus H. Strong, *Systematic Theology* (Westwood, N.J: Revell, 1907), 789.

[15] Erikson, 650.

Armianism

While statements of the Arminian view vary to some degree, their starting point is the concept that God desires all persons to be saved.[16] They point to the definite assertions of the scripture stating that the Lord does not want "that any should perish, but that all should reach repentance."[17] Moreover, they believe that God's grace is given by God to all persons indiscriminately. Arminians argue with regard to Romans 8:29 that those who are predestined by God are those who in his infinite knowledge, He is able to foresee that they will accept the offer of salvation made in Jesus Christ.[18]

A second major conception of Arminianism is that all persons are able to believe or to meet the condition of salvation. If this were not the case, the universal invitation to salvation would make little sense. John Wesley and others, speak about "prevenient grace" given by God to all persons indiscriminately so that everyone is capable of accepting the offer of salvation.

Depravity and Free Will

The writer generally argues for a Wesleyan-Arminian theology relating to the question of depravity. One the one hand, the writer disagrees with Pelagius' concept that mankind with "his free choice" and own efforts, is able to fulfil God's commands. Both Luther and Calvin are right in asserting that fallen humans are not free in regards to achieving their own salvation.[19] Mankind needs God's grace in order to respond to his offer. No free human act can move toward God or do any spiritual good without the aid of God's Grace.

One the other hand, the writer disagrees with the Calvinist concept of total depravity. There is no indication that after Adam sinned and became spiritually dead[20] and a sinner "by nature"[21] that he became so depraved that he could neither hear the voice of God nor make any free response to God's words.[22] While the Bible speaks about fallen man as ignorant, depraved, and a slave of sin, it also assures that man deliberately "suppresses" the truth (Romans 1:18-19), and is under the power of Satan by a free act of "disobedience"

---

[16] Samuel Wakefield, *A complete System of Christian Theology* (Cincinnati: Hitchcock & Walden, 1869), 387.
[17] 2 Peter 3:9
[18] Erikson, 301.
[19] Martin Luther, *The Bondage of the Will,* trans. Henry Cole (Grand Rapids, Mich.: Baker Book House, 1967), 79.
[20] Gen. 2:17; Eph. 2:1 and others.
[21] Eph. 2:3

(Eph. 2:2). In short, God makes his grace available to any person, but the sinner must, with his infirm will, cooperate with this grace in order to be regenerated.[23]

---

[22] Gen. 3:19-10, Gen. 3:9-10, Gen. 9:6, James 3:9 and many more.
[23] Sproul, 78.

Election

Predestination and Human Freedom

By looking at the question of predestination man must confess that with a human mind he will never fully comprehend these divine mysteries. If there were not so many passages of scripture where one reads about God's will that all be saved, man's disability to bring divine predestination and human free will to a common denominator, man would come to the conclusion of double predestination, just as Calvin has.[24]

However, from the perspective of the parable of the marriage of the King's Son in Matthew 22, one sees that humans must accept God's calling (in reversal, repentance and conversion). Whoever does not assume God's offer is not part of the chosen, and will fare like the man who can not stand up to the king without wedding dress (Matthew 22:12). Despite the man's appointment to the Kingdom of Heaven, he is lost. The Parable ends by stating that: "many are called, but few are chosen," (Matthew 22.14). The writer agrees with Donald Guthrie's Conclusion, that the chosen ones are those who have truly accepted the invitation.[25]

Before Knowledge of God

A comparison of passages regarding election with passages that command conversion shows that God's predestination does not take place independently of human decision.[26] To man's limited, fleshly understanding, the concept of "before knowledge"[27] or "before seeing" is the same as the "providence of God" and can more easily be comprehended. The writer has demonstrated that the concept of election is always connected with human free will. God's election is never an edict. By looking at the question of "accepting or rejecting the grace of God" the writer therefore disagrees with the Calvinist concept of unconditional election.

---

[24] Erich Mauerhofer, *Course outline for Soteriologie* (Theologische Hochschule Basel, Basel 2007), 43.

[25] Donald Guthrie, *New Testament Theology* (Illinois: Inter- Varsity Press, 1981), 85.

[26] Mauerhofer, 43. / See for example Revelation 13:8 and Revelation 3:5.

[27] Romans 8:29 (NKJV)

Salvation / Chosen by God and Chosen by Man

It has been said, that on the outside of the door of heaven it reads, "Whosoever will may enter," while on the inside is written, "I have chosen you before the foundation of the world". [28] "Chosen but free" - both are according to scripture true and therefore, along with the Trinity and the Incarnation, one of the great mysteries of Christian faith.[29] While the writer generally agrees with a Wesleyan-Arminian theology, he disagrees with Arminius in that election is the result of a human act.[30] The writer believes that human logic humbly needs to accept that the Bible holds no contradiction between God's sovereignty, or predetermination, and human freedom to choose. (In the attachment there is more explanation regarding this thought.)

---

[28] Geisler, 38.

[29] Ibid, 38

[30] Florian Sonderheimer, *Course outline Sot. 5-2*, Buchegg Bibelschule, Zürich, 2006, 2.

CONCLUSION

This essay, derived from different viewpoints, that man has a significant free will. On this assumption, it is clear that man is entirely responsible to accept or reject the grace of God.

Firstly, the writer illustrated that divine sovereignty does not exclude a significant free will. To argue against a concept of free will, would automatically charge God to be the cause of evil. Secondly, the writer argued for a Wesleyan-Arminian theology of depravity, which depicts the image of God in fallen humanity as effaced but not erased. According to this view, everyone is able to respond to the grace of God by accepting or rejecting the gospel of salvation. Lastly, the writer observed that the concept of election is always connected with human personal freedom of decision. God's election is never an edict.

In conclusion, the reality of free will goes to the heart of Christian anthropology.[31] Otherwise, mankind's moral agency would perish and man would be reduced to a sham, a mere chimera with no substantive reality. The writer must conclude that: "… millions of men, without any preceding offence or fault of theirs, were unchangeably doomed to everlasting burnings![32]

While rejecting strong Calvinism, the writer humbly confesses that "Chosen but free," as well as the relationship between divine sovereignty and human free will, rests a wonderful secret not fully comprehendible to human logic.

---

[31] Sproul, 28.
[32] The Sermons of John Wesley, 1872 Edition (Thomas Jackson, editor) *SERMON ONE HUNDRED TWENTY-EIGHT Free Grace* Preached at Bristol, in the year 1740.

ATTACHMENT

Predetermined and Freely Chosen

Following the writer exemplarily chose some biblical references that indicate that the Bible holds no contradiction between God's predetermination and human free choice.

Acts 2:23 on the one hand declares that Jesus' death was determined "by God's set purpose and foreknowledge." On the other hand, Jesus says he did it freely: "No one takes it from me, but I lay it down of my own accord" (John 10:17-18). Noting could be clearer. God determined it from all eternity, and yet Jesus did it freely. If it is true of Jesus' free choices, then there is no contradiction in asserting that free actions are both determined and free.

Luke 22:22 says about Jesus' betrayal: "Truly the Son of man goeth, as it was determined: but woe unto that man by whom he is betrayed!" God determined that the betrayal must happen, but when it occurred, it did so as a result of a free and responsible act of Judas.

John 6:37 describes, "All that the Father gave me will come to me, and whoever comes to me I will never drive away." On the one hand, only those preordained to do so will come to Christ. (John 6:44). On the other hand, it is also true that "whoever" chooses to come will be saved (Rom. 10:13).

In conclusion, the Bible holds no contradiction between God's predetermination and human free choice.

BIBLIOGRAPHY

Basinger, David, and Randall Basinger, eds. *Predestination & Free Will.* Downers Grove, IL: InterVarsity Press, 1986.

Brand, Chad Owen ed. *Perspectives on Election: 5 Views.* Nashville, TN: Broadman & Holman Publishers, 2006.

Erikson, Millard. *Introducing Christian Doctrine.* Grand Rapids, MI: Backer Academic, 2005.

Geisler, Normen L. *Chosen but free: A Balanced view of divine election.* Grand Rapids, MI: Baker Publishing Group, 2001.

Hoekema, Anthony. *Saved by Grace.* Grand Rapids: MI Eerdmans, 1989.

Luther, Martin. *The Bondage of the Will,* trans. Henry Cole. Grand Rapids, MI: Baker Book House, 1967.

Marshall, Howard. *Kept by the Power of God*: A Study of Perseverance and Falling Away. Carlistle: Paternoster Press, 1995.

Mauerhofer, Erich. *Course outline Soteriologie*, Theologische Hochschule Basel, 2007.

Moody, Dale. *The Word of Truth: A Summary of Christian Doctrine Based on Biblical Revelation.* Grand Rapids: Eerdmans, 1981.

Peters, Benedikt. *George Whitefield: Der Erwecker Englands und Amerikas.* Bielefeld, DE: CLV, 1997.

Picirilli, Robert. *Grace, Faith, Free Will: Contrasting Views of Savation: Calvinism and Arminianism.* Nashville, TN: Randall House Publications, 2002.

Sonderheimer, Florian. *Course outline* Sot. 5-2, Buchegg Bibelschule, Zürich, 2006.

Sproul, R.C. *Willing to believe: The Controversy over Free Will.* Grand Rapids, MI: Baker Books, 1997.

Strong, H Augustus. *Systematic Theology.* Westwood, N.J: Revell, 1907.

Thiessen, Jacob. *Biblische Glaubenslehre: Eine Systematische Theologie für jedermann.* Plata, Paraguay: Verlag der Bibelschule Loma Plata, 2003.

Wakefield, Samuel. *A complete System of Christian Theology.* Cincinnati: Hitchcock & Walden, 1869.

Wilder-Smith, Arthur E. *Ist das ein Gott der Liebe.* Neuhausen, DE: Hänssler, 1988.